HERE'S
TO THE
GRADUATE

MARIANNE RICHMOND

Published by Sourcebooks, Inc.
P.O. Box 4410, Naperville, Illinois 60567-4410
(630) 961-3900
Fax: (630) 961-2168
www.sourcebooks.com

Printed and bound in China.
LEO 10 9 8 7 6 5 4 3 2 1

To:_____

From: _____

Congrats Graduate!
Did you think this
day would *ever* come?

Now, what's next?
As you begin your
next adventure, I want to
send with you my wishes…

I wish you

GUTS.

Challenge your ability
by trying something new,
even if you're scared.
Or nervous.
Or about to throw up.

I wish you

a generous

heart.

Share your time and resources
with others,

don't expect anything in return,

and watch
your good fortune

GROW!

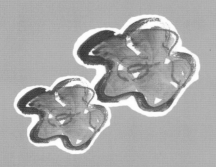

I wish you a

playful spirit.

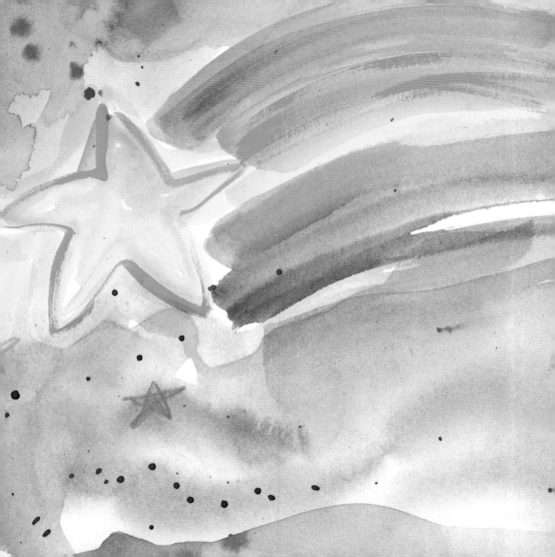

Remember that it's always cool to dance,

master the monkey bars,

spin a cartwheel,

wish upon a star,

hug your mom or dad,

befriend a child,

or hand out Halloween candy.

I wish you

humility.

One of the greatest gifts you can give is to be genuinely interested in another's life.

Ask questions

and listen *more*

than you talk.

I wish you

patience with others.

Seems like everything

takes longer than you hope.

A boss can be downright annoying.

Traffic is crazy.

People are rude.

Take a deep breath before you blow.

I wish you patience with yourself, too. Give it your all and give yourself a break.

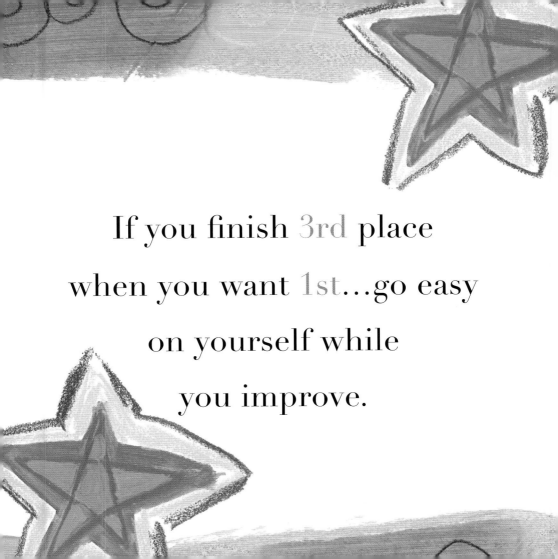

If you finish 3rd place when you want 1st...go easy on yourself while you improve.

I wish you determination.
Some things will come easy.
A lot won't.

Whatever your goal,
remind yourself why
it's important

...and keep going!

I wish you
great friendships.

Surround yourself with loving,
supportive, funny friends

and tell them how much
you appreciate them!

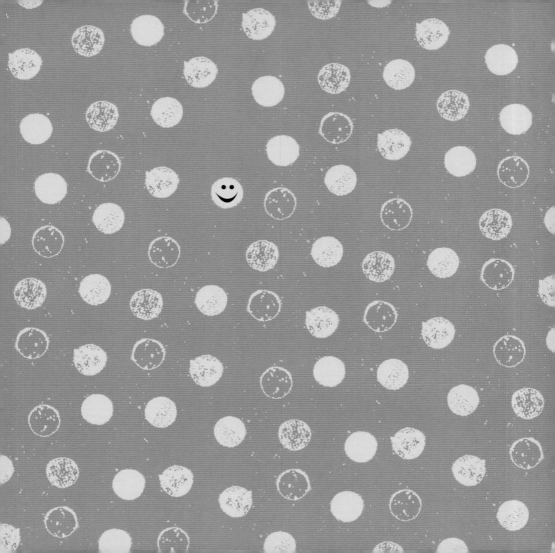

I wish you
a great sense
of humor.

If you can find the fun in life,

you'll find the
journey much

more entertaining!

I wish you an

opinion.

What do you think about
this or that?
Do you agree or disagree?
Speak up and
state your case!

I wish you
an open mind.

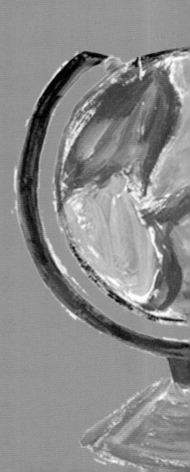

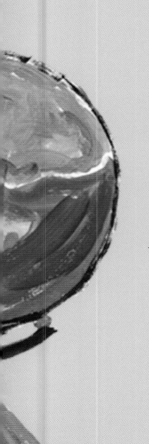

Appreciate others'
ideas, ways, customs,
and preferences.
Acceptance cultivates
kindness.

I wish you

common sense.

When faced with situations,
decisions, quandaries, and questions,
consult your experiences and instincts
and try to respond with good judgment.

I wish you curiosity.

Keep asking, keep trying, keep learning, keep living.

I wish you
honesty.

It's hard sometimes to

hear AND tell the truth.

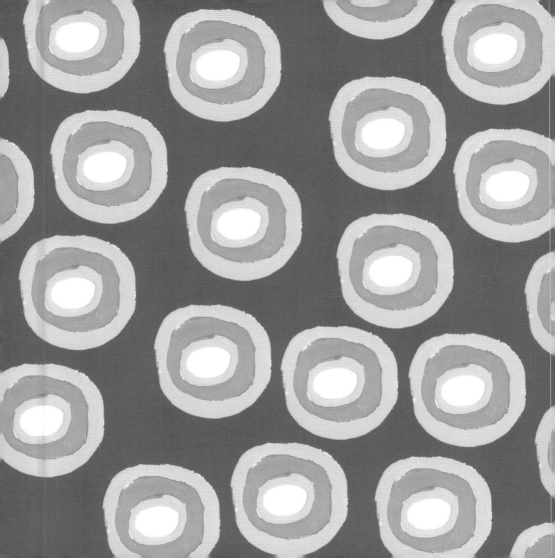

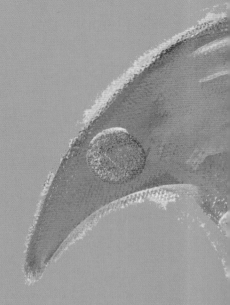

Do it with gentleness and
tact, however, and you will

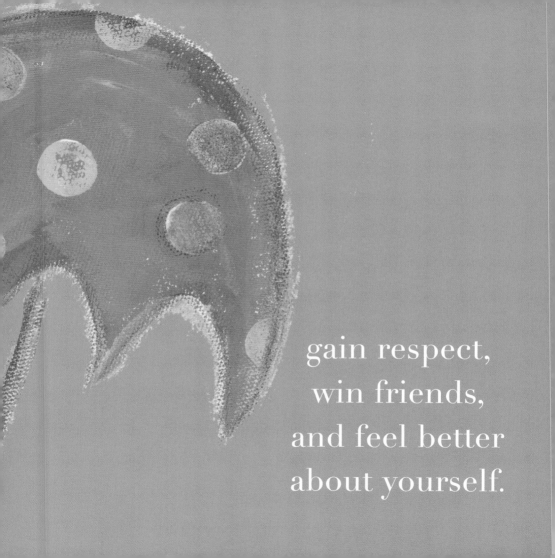

gain respect,
win friends,
and feel better
about yourself.

I wish you

self-respect.

Do you like you?

WE do!

Do you know your limits, values, and absolutes? A strong moral compass will be your ultimate guide through life.

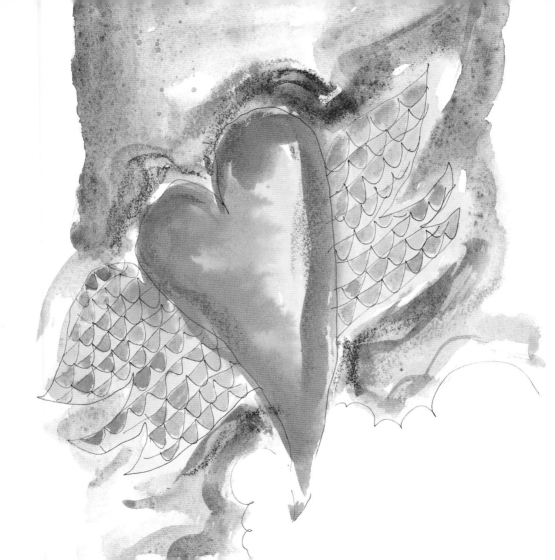

I wish you joyfulness!

Laugh often.

Plan surprises.

Be spontaneous.

Tell jokes.

Be silly.

GOOD
LUCk!

Lastly,
I wish you
luck.

For all the

planning, striving,

and learning we do,

there's no
substitute for
great timing **and** pure luck!

Congratulations,

Graduate!

About the Author

Beloved author and illustrator Marianne Richmond has touched the lives of millions for nearly two decades through her award-winning books, greeting cards, and other gift products that offer people the most heartfelt way to connect with each other. She lives in the Minneapolis area. Visit www.marianne richmond.com.